Ring-a-Ding

Alphabet Soup

A Phonics Reader

By Sasha Quinton

The Book Shop, Ltd.
New York, New York

© 2009 The Book Shop, Ltd
Photographs © Juniperimages Corporation

Furry friends, both small and **big,**
Come to dance and **sing.**

They bark and meow a **silly** song.
They **spin.** They **dip.** They **swing.**

woof

woof

Ring-a-ding-ding. Three pups bark.
They woof, bow-wow, and **yip.**

Two **pretty** birds **twitter** a tune.
They chirp and tweet. They're **hip.**

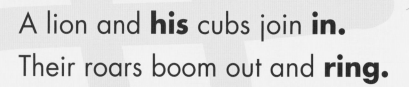

A lion and **his** cubs join **in.**
Their roars boom out and **ring.**

A **hippo** makes a mighty noise,
While three **little kittens sing.**

Four fluffy **chicks skip** and **spin.**
They **flip** and flap their **wings.**

Then a panda does a **silly jig,**
While a **little lizard swings.**

Clippety-clop. Three horses dance.
They rear up, buck, and **kick.**

Clickety-clack. They **click** their hooves.
Their three tails **swish** and **flick.**

One **little kitten** steals the show.
She loves to dance. She **dips.**

The **kitten spins** around and around.
She twirls. She **twists.** She **flips.**

A big **chimp** tries to **spin** like her.
He can't! The poor **chimp trips.**

Bing-bang! He's down. He **hits** the floor.
The **chimp** then slides and **slips.**

It's so much fun! They all join **in.**
Ring-a-ding-ding! They slide and **sing!**